press against its walls full

ender that grows serenely of

e, and savory, whose blossom

n sage and lads-love, that a

ry a yellowed page. Woodru

e lovely, lovelier still are

n garden with a loveliness de

e rightly. Ancient centuries

easure rightly. Ancient cent

th is lost in fragrance of the

Basil, rosemary, marjoram are

eside a dripping pool. There

knew and pressed for us in

araway, and rue. Old flowe

ar box and cedar trees. I kn

see or indrawn breath can m

PRESENTED TO

_____

FROM

_____

DATE

Poems for Gardeners

A JOYFUL BOUQUET

WATERCOLORS BY
JO ANNA POEHLMANN

IDEALS PUBLICATIONS
NASHVILLE, TENNESSEE

ISBN 0-8249-4301-5

Published by Ideals Publications, a division of Guideposts
535 Metroplex Drive, Suite 250, Nashville, Tennessee 37211
www.idealspublications.com

Caseside printed in the U.S.A.
Text printed and bound in Mexico.
Printed by RR Donnelley & Sons.
Color separations by Precision Color Graphics, Franklin, Wisconsin.

Library of Congress Cataloging-in-Publication Data
Poems for gardeners : a joyful bouquet / watercolors by Jo Anna Poehlmann.
    p. cm.
Includes index.
    ISBN 0-8249-4301-5 (alk. paper)
  1. Gardens--Poetry. 2. Gardening--Poetry. 3. American poetry. 4. English
poetry.   I. Ideals Publishing Corp.

  PS595.G33 P636 2001
    811.008'0364--dc21

10 9 8 7 6 5 4 3 2 1   2001006978

POEMS SELECTED BY JULIE K. HOGAN
DESIGNED BY EVE DEGRIE

ACKNOWLEDGMENTS

BOISSEAU, MICHELLE. "Potato" from *Spud Songs: An Anthology of Potato Poems*. Copyright © 1999 by Michelle Boisseau. Reprinted by permission of Helicon Nine Editions. COTTON, JOHN. "Pumpkins" from *Old Movies*. Published by Chatto & Windus. Used by permission of the author. PIERCY, MARGE. "The Love of Lettuce" from *Circles on the Water*. Copyright © 1982 by Marge Piercy. Used by permission of Alfred A. Knopf, a division of Random House, Incorporated. ROETHKE, THEODORE. "Transplanting" from *The Collected Poems of Theodore Roethke*. Copyright © 1948 by Theodore Roethke. Used by permission of Doubleday, a division of Random House. SATHOFF, CRAIG E. "Garden Harvest." Used by permission of Mary L. Sathoff. STUART, MURIEL. "The Seed Shop" from *Selected Poems*. Published by Jonathan Cape. Used by permission of Elizabeth Stapleforth. UNDERHILL, RUTH H. "Harvesttime." Used by permission of the author. Our sincere thanks to the following authors whom we were unable to locate: Reginald Arkell for "What Is a Garden?"; Mazie V. Caruthers for "Gardens"; Thomas Curtis Clark for "Who Hath a Garden"; Catherine Cate Coblentz for "Herb Garden"; Leonard Feeney for "The Geranium"; Nell K. A. Foster for "Campaign"; Earl J. Grant for "Summer, Country Style"; Edith Sitwell for "The Innocent Spring"; Arthur Symons for "The Gardener."

CONTENTS

THE GARDEN
SEASONS

IN THE GARDEN

New feet within my garden go,
New fingers stir the sod;
A troubadour upon the elm
Betrays the solitude.

New children play upon the green,
New weary sleep below;
And still the pensive spring returns,
And still the punctual snow!
—EMILY DICKINSON

THE INNOCENT SPRING

In the great gardens, after bright spring rain,
We find sweet innocence come once again,
White periwinkles, little pensionnaires,
With muslin gowns and shy and candid airs,

That under saint-blue skies, with gold stars sown,
Hide their sweet innocence by spring winds blown,
From zephyr libertines that like Richelieu
And d'Orsay their gold-spangled kisses blew;

And lilies of the valley whose buds blonde and tight
Seem curls of little schoolchildren that light
The priests' procession, when on some saint's day
Along the country paths they make their way;

Forget-me-nots, whose eyes of childish blue,
God-starred like heaven, speak of love still true;
And all the flowers that we call "dear heart,"
Who say their prayers like children, then depart

Into the dark. Amid the dew's bright beams
The summer airs, like Weber waltzes, fall
Round the first rose who, flushed with her youth, seems
Like a young Princess dressed for her first ball.

Who knows what beauty ripens from dark mould
After the sad wind and the winter's cold? —
But a small wind sighed, colder than the rose
Blooming in desolation, "No one knows."
— EDITH SITWELL

THE FIRST BLUEBIRD

Jest rain and snow! and rain again!
    And dribble! drip! and blow!
Then snow! and thaw! and slush! and then—
    Some more rain and snow!

This morning I was 'most afeard
    To wake up—when, I jing!
I seen the sun shine out and heerd
    The first bluebird of spring!
Mother she'd raised the winder some;
And in acrost the orchard come,
    Soft as an angel's wing,
A breezy, treesy, beesy hum,
    Too sweet for any thing!

The winter's shroud was rent apart—
  The sun bust forth in glee,
And when that bluebird sung, my hart
  Hopped out o' bed with me!
—JAMES WHITCOMB RILEY

SPRING ARITHMETIC

It was the busy hour of four
When from the city hardware store
Emerged a gentleman, who bore
One hoe, one spade, one wheelbarrow.

From there our hero promptly went
Into a seed establishment,
And for these things his money spent:
One peck of bulbs, one job-lot shrub,
    one quart assorted seeds.

He has a garden under way,
And if he's fairly lucky, say,
He'll have, about the end of May,
One squash vine, one eggplant, one radish.

—AUTHOR UNKNOWN

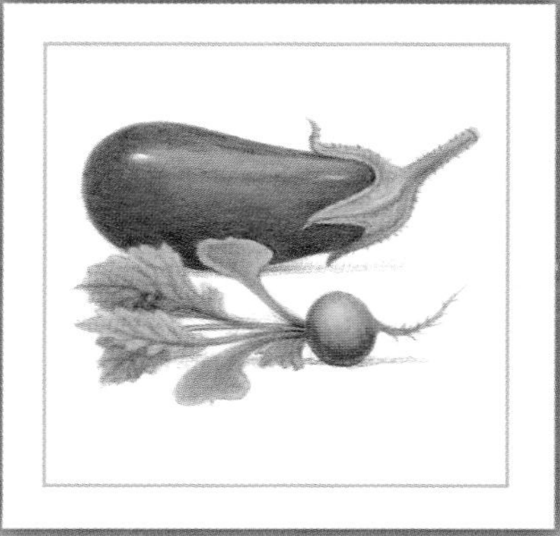

CAMPAIGN

The first maneuver—a crocus showed,
Its bright flare starting the episode.
A busy signaling butterfly
Handled two flags against the sky.

And then the plane of a bird revealed
That hosts of spring were in the field.
Little breezes advanced en masse —
In one direction moved the grass.

Through the boughs, as the sunlight pranced,
A regiment of buds advanced.
Down in the orchard, guarded with wire,
Cherry artillery opened fire.

And heroes raised on the glowing turf
The oriflamme of a great rebirth.
With a volley of rain they charged the hills
And won the top with daffodils.
— NELL K. A. FOSTER

THE SEED SHOP

Here in a quiet and dusty room they lie,
Faded as a crumbled stone or shifting sand,
Forlorn as ashes, shrivelled, scentless, dry—
  Meadows and gardens running through my hand.

  In this brown husk a dale of hawthorn dreams,
  A cedar in this narrow cell is thrust;
It will drink deeply of a century's streams,
These lilies shall make summer on my dust.

Here in their safe and simple house of death,
Sealed in their shell a million roses leap;
Here I can blow a garden with my breath,
And in my hand a forest lies asleep.
—MURIEL STUART

NEW-TURNED SOIL

The smell of new-turned garden soil
Is in the air. With patient toil
The musk of earth is freed
From winter's cell . . .
Each shovelful is like an urn
Diffusing redolent odor;
A freshness comes with each upturn
Of living earth . . .
A scent a rose may not excel.

—ALICE PROKASKY

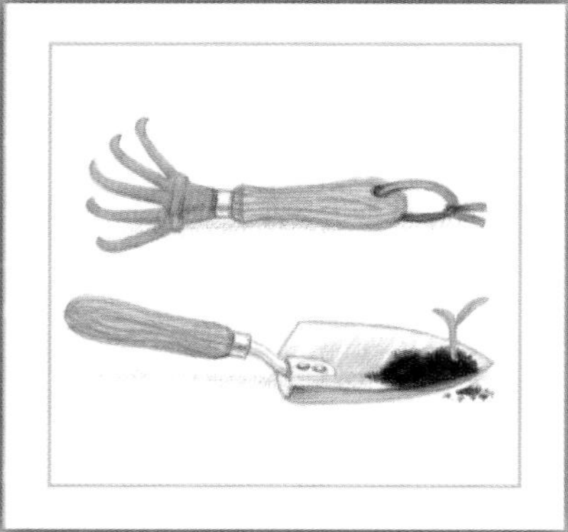

ARTISTRY

Glad summertime is graced with artistry
Of flowers in multi-rhythmed tracery
Like fragile balls of white and purple phlox,
And blushing faces of tall hollyhocks;
Long spears of foxglove reaching high
And meadow daisies laughing at the sky;
Bright flares of asters, charming and sedate,
And shy petunias by the garden gate,
Red roses throwing perfume to the breeze
While honeysuckle caters to the bees.
The morning glories awaken with the sun
And four-o'clocks tell when the day is done.
These are the strokes of life and hope, the lines
Glad summertime artistically designs.

— HAROLD A. SCHULZ

HARVESTTIME AGAIN

It seems like only yesterday
That we readied the rich black soil
And planted each tiny seedling,
Beginning the springtime toil.

The refreshing little silver drops
Of gentle springtime rain
Watered the thirsty tender shoots
Till the sun came out again.

All of summer they swiftly grew
Reaching higher up each day,
While lovingly we tended them
In a careful tender way.

Now already the harvest
Is ripe and ready to reap,
We'll carefully tuck it safely away
To use when winter is cold and deep.
—RUTH H. UNDERHILL

GARDEN IN WINTER

My garden is all put to bed for the winter.
Faded and dead are its bright-colored blossoms,
Its green leaves are turned to dull brown.
But deep in the dark soil the dry bulbs

And the delicate rootlets are sleeping;
While the snow makes a blanket above them,
They sleep and they wait for the spring's
First call to awakening life.

Sometimes when dark days are burdened;
When my hands are wearied with working;
I wish that some kindly gardener
Would cover me warm, and leave me to rest

Like the roots and the bulbs in my garden—
To sleep and grow strong like the flowers
For another season of blooming.

—DOROTHY WHITEHEAD HOUGH

The First Dandelion

Simple and fresh and fair from winter's close emerging,
As if no artifice of fashion, business, politics,
    has ever been,
Forth from its sunny nook of shelter'd grass—
Innocent, golden, calm as the dawn,
The spring's first dandelion shows its trustful face.
— Walt Whitman

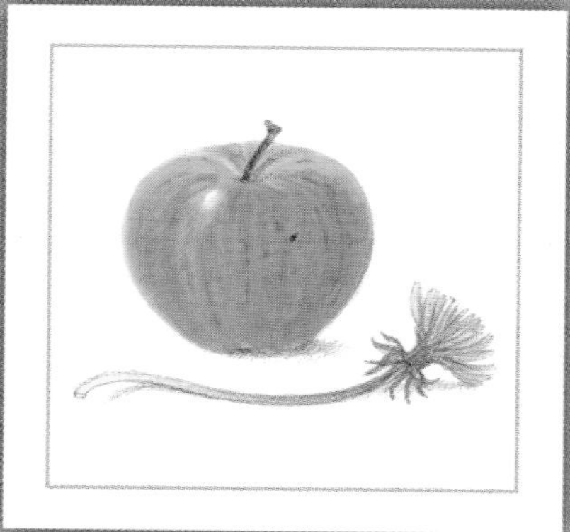

FLOWER CHORUS

O such a commotion under the ground,
When March called, "Ho, there! ho!"
Such spreading of rootlets far and wide,
Such whisperings to and fro!

"Are you ready?" the Snowdrop asked,
" 'Tis time to start, you know."
"Almost, my dear!" the Scilla replied,
"I'll follow as soon as you go."

Then "Ha! ha! ha!" a chorus came
Of laughter sweet and low,
From millions of flowers under the ground,
Yes, millions beginning to grow.

"I'll promise my blossoms," the Crocus said,
"When I hear the blackbird sing."

And straight thereafter Narcissus cried,
"My silver and gold I'll bring."

"And ere they are dulled," another spoke,
"The Hyacinth bells shall ring."
But the Violet only murmured, "I'm here,"
And sweet grew the air of spring.

Then "Ha! ha! ha!" a chorus came
Of laughter sweet and low,
From millions of flowers under the ground,
Yes, millions beginning to grow.

And well may they cheerily laugh "Ha! ha!"
In laughter sweet and low,
The millions of flowers under the ground,
Yes, millions beginning to grow.
— RALPH WALDO EMERSON

Seed-Time Hymn

Lord, in Thy name Thy servants plead
    And Thou hast sworn to hear;
Thine is the harvest, Thine the seed,
    The fresh and fading year;

Our hope, when autumn winds blew wild,
    We trusted, Lord, with Thee;
And still, now spring has on us smiled,
    We wait on Thy decree.

The former and the latter rain,
    The summer sun and air,
The green ear, and the golden grain,
    All Thine, are ours by prayer.

Thine too by right, and ours by grace,
  The wondrous growth unseen,
The hopes that soothe, the fears that brace,
  The love that shines serene.

So grant the precious things brought forth
  By sun and moon below,
That Thee in Thy new heaven and earth
  We never may forego.
—JOHN KEBLE

A Gardener's
Hands and
Heart

Who Loves a Garden

Who loves a garden
Finds within his soul
Life's whole;
He hears the anthem of the soil
While ingrates toil;
And sees beyond his little sphere
The waving fronds of heaven, clear.

— Louise Seymour Jones

GIVE ME THE SPLENDID SILENT SUN

Give me the splendid silent sun
   with all its beams full-dazzling,
Give me juicy autumnal fruit ripe and red
   from the orchard,
Give me a field where the unmowed grass grows,
Give me an arbor, give me the trellised grape,
Give me fresh corn and wheat, give me
   serene-moving animals teaching content.

Give me nights perfectly quiet as on high
    plateaus west of the Mississippi, and I am
    looking up at the stars,
Give me, odorous at sunrise, a garden of
    beautiful flowers where I can walk undisturbed.
—WALT WHITMAN

THE GARDENER

At evening, I have seen him wander in
And out between the hedges;
On the moss he treads, where shadows spin
A misty web. He skirts the edges
Indistinct of heliotrope and jessamine.

I wonder what he does, studious
And furtive in the gloom.
Is he covering the tremulous
Young plants that have no spreading bloom
When night is cool, to keep them young and luminous?

Or is he mutely speculating there
Upon the flowers themselves;
His love observing them through the veiled air
As plain as when he weeds and delves
At noon, but with more secret and more wistful care?

I call the garden mine. This votary
Who loves it makes it his;
A poet owns his legend. If I were
To ask the garden whose it is,
It would reply: "My master is this gardener."
— GLADYS CROMWELL

THE GARDENER

The gardener in his old brown hands
Turns over the brown earth,
As if he loves and understands
The flowers before their birth,
The fragile little childish strands
He buries in the earth.
Like pious children, one by one,
He sets them head by head,
And draws the clothes, when all is done,
Closely about each head;
And leaves his children to sleep on
In the one, quiet bed.

— ARTHUR SYMONS

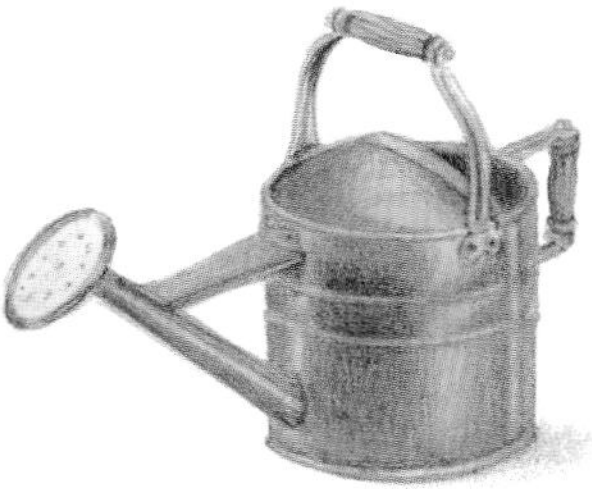

Transplanting

Watching hands transplanting,
Turning and tamping,
Lifting the young plants with two fingers,
Sifting in a palm-full of fresh loam,
One swift movement,
Then plumping in the bunched roots,
A single twist of the thumbs, a tamping and turning,
All in one,
Quick on the wooden bench,
A shaking down, while the stem stays straight,
Once, twice, and a faint third thump,

Into the flat-box it goes,
Ready for the long days under the sloped glass:

The sun warming the fine loam,
The young horns winding and unwinding,
Creaking their thin spines,
The underleaves, the smallest buds
Breaking into nakedness,
The blossoms extending
Out into the sweet air,
The whole flower extending outward,
Stretching and reaching.
—THEODORE ROETHKE

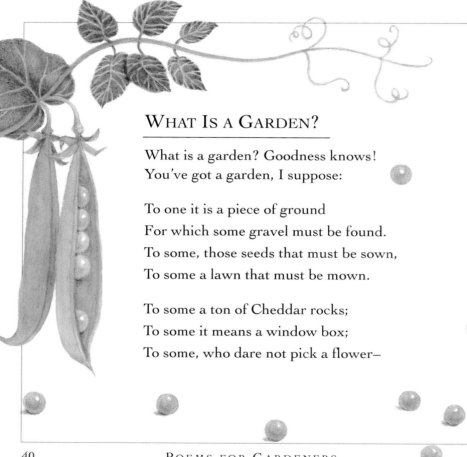

WHAT IS A GARDEN?

What is a garden? Goodness knows!
You've got a garden, I suppose:

To one it is a piece of ground
For which some gravel must be found.
To some, those seeds that must be sown,
To some a lawn that must be mown.

To some a ton of Cheddar rocks;
To some it means a window box;
To some, who dare not pick a flower–

POEMS FOR GARDENERS

A man, at eighteen pence an hour.
To some, it is a silly jest
About the latest garden pest;
To some, a haven where they find
Forgetfulness and peace of mind . . .

What is a garden, large or small
'Tis just a garden, after all.
—REGINALD ARKELL

GARDENS

What pure delight a garden brings!
What joy in watching growing things
    Upspringing from the sodden mold
    Their wealth of beauty to unfold—
'Tis here my spirit soars and sings!

To note the flash of painted wings,
And hark the bees' soft murmurings
    In quest of sweets the blossoms hold;
    Where all gray days are days of gold,
Strolling its paths bright wanderings,
      What pure delight!

—LOUELLA C. POOLE

WHO HATH A GARDEN

Who hath a garden, he has joy,
However small his plot may be.
Wide his horizons; in his demesne
Master of beauty and life is he.

God has gracious smiled on him,
    Made him a helper in His great task—
Building a glorious world in time;
    What finer task could any one ask?

Who hath a garden, he has friends—
    Lilies and roses will not forsake;
When they depart, 'tis but for a time;
    They will return when the spring winds wake.

Let him rejoice on his kingly throne
    Who hath a garden of pink and gold;
Kings bear burdens and soon are gray—
    Who hath a garden shall not grow old.
    —THOMAS CURTIS CLARK

RIOTOUS GARDEN

I love my old riotous garden,
　　Its unconcern gladdens the heart;
No method whate'er in its beauty,
　　For nature supreme reigns in art.

Each path leads to some spot enchanting,
　　Full fragrant with prodigal bloom,
Where robins, gay, warble approval,
　　In carols dispersing all gloom.

To entertain angels and fairies
　　Seems just the correct thing to do,
They're always so loving and gentle,
　　With hearts blessed by charity true.

Here beautiful thoughts without pattern,
　　Where God sheds His blessing divine,
Form poems from nebulous nothings
　　In this riotous garden of mine.
—JULIE CAROLINE O'HARA

GARDENS

My garden goes to rest at night.
   To wind-sweet lullabies
The flowers fold them in their slim
   Green shifts and close their eyes.
Over their nodding heads the Moon
   Her tranquil vigil keeps—
Oh, 'tis a peaceful sight to see
   A garden when it sleeps!
When through gray morning mists the sun
   Rides splendidly to view,
The flowers flutter drowsy lids
   All sweet and wet with dew!
Refreshed by slumber, every one
   Its dainty toilet makes—
Oh, 'tis a lovely thing to see
   A garden when it wakes!
— MAZIE V. CARUTHERS

IF GOD GAVE ME A GARDEN

If God gave me a garden
  Where phlox and poppies grew,
With china pinks and heart's-ease
  And larkspur's June-time blue,
All other ills I'd pardon,
  Content with thorn and rue,
If God gave me a garden
  Where bluebells caught the dew.

If God gave me for treasure,
  One tiny, precious plot,
So sweet with dainty daphne,
  And shy forget-me-not,

I'd want no other pleasure,
    Nor envy richer lot,
If God gave me for treasure,
    One wee, rose-circled spot.
—BERNICE MILDRED ELKINS

My Garden Is a Pleasant Place

My garden is a pleasant place
Of sun glory and leaf grace.
There is an ancient cherry tree
Where yellow warblers sing to me,
And an old grape arbor, where
A robin builds her nest, and there
Above the lima beans and peas
She croons her little melodies,
Her blue eggs hidden in the green
Fastness of that leafy screen.
Here are striped zinnias that bees
Fly far to visit; and sweet peas,
Like little butterflies newborn,
And over by the tasseled corn
Are sunflowers and hollyhocks,
And pink and yellow four-o'clocks.

Here are hummingbirds that come
To seek the tall delphinium—
Songless bird and scentless flower
Communing in a golden hour.

My garden is a pleasant place
Of moon glory and wind grace.
O friend, wherever you may be,
Will you not come to visit me?
Over fields and streams and hills,
I'll pipe like yellow daffodils,
And every little wind that blows
Shall take my message as it goes.
A heart may travel very far
To come where its desires are,
Oh, may some power touch my ear,
And grant me grace, and make you hear!
—LOUISE DRISCOLL

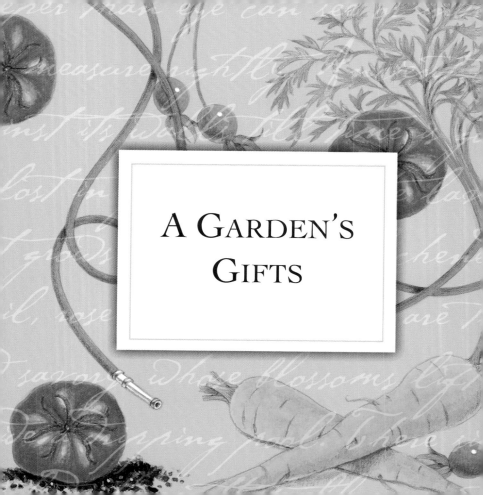

A GARDEN'S GIFTS

A GARDEN SPOT

A garden spot may be a noisy place
Where droning bees
Seek honey, spiders weave their silver lace
Upon the trees,
And little birds sing songs the livelong day.

Or it may be so silent that it seems
The flowers sleep,
And shy, mysterious virgin dreams
Their vigil keep,
And God communes with earth the livelong day.
— PRINGLE BARRET

GARDEN HARVEST

What pageantry of color
And what beauty so sublime
Have found their way right to my door
This lovely harvesttime!

Tomatoes huge and luscious red
Are ripe to slice and eat,
And golden pumpkins for a pie
Will be a special treat.

POEMS FOR GARDENERS

The onion garlands hang in wait
Beside the peppers green
While carrots, beans, and ruby beets
Add their hues to the scene.

In baskets waiting at my door
They are a grand display
Of wondrous harvest that will be
A boon on wintry days.
—CRAIG E. SATHOFF

A GARDEN'S GIFTS

SUMMER, COUNTRY STYLE

Tawny golden peaches,
Crimson roses, too;
Blue morning glories
Drenched in sparkling dew.

Plump watermelons,
Green-gold cantaloupes;
Rosy crepe myrtles
Festooning clay slopes.

POEMS FOR GARDENERS

Sweet honeysuckles
Twining up fence rails;
Mist like gray chiffon
Draping hills in veils.

Rare stained-window skies,
Green corn, mile on mile . . .
All of these make up
Summer, country style!
—EARLE J. GRANT

A GARDEN

Hollyhocks, showing off pink ruffled dresses,
Gossip together on tall, furry stalks,
Coyly ignoring the bachelor buttons
Peeping at them from behind the red phlox.

Lilacs combine with the sweet white alyssum
To fill the warm air with their heady perfume,
And noisy bees gather the generous off'rings
Of all the fair flowers that come into bloom.

And up in a treetop, enjoying the garden,
And adding his part to the beauty below,
A mockingbird sings with creative abandon
A love song to everything summer can grow.

— LINNEA BODMAN

POTATO

I don't want trouble, but the rutabagas
and the turnips, especially the turnips,
are muttering Ingrate, Upstart, and throwing
me looks. Sheez, Louise. I'm hardly escarole.
So I got lots of friends? I'm adaptable,
a hard worker, and I don't ask favors.
Put them in a basket and they're bitter.
Put them in a pan, better be copper.
The butter's too pale, the pepper's too coarse.
On and on. With me if I'm forgotten
I turn extra-spective and gregarious.
I'm not called the Dirt Apple for nothing.
I stick my necks out at any warm chink
and grope for the garden on leafy legs.
—MICHELLE BOISSEAU

THE TRYST

Potato was deep in the dark under ground,
    Tomato, above in the light.
The little Tomato was ruddy and round,
    The little Potato was white.

And redder and redder she rounded above,
    And paler and paler he grew,
And neither suspected a mutual love
    Till they met in a Brunswick stew.
—JOHN BANISTER TABB

THE LOVE OF LETTUCE

With a pale green curly
lust I gloat over it nestled
there on the wet earth
(oakleaf, buttercrunch, ruby, cos)
like so many nests
waiting for birds
who lay hard-boiled eggs.
The first green eyes
of the mustard, the frail
wands of carrots, the fat
thrust of the peas: all
are precious as I kneel
in the mud weeding
and the thinnings go into the salad.

The garden with crooked
wandering rows dug
by the three of us
drunk with sunshine has
an intricate pattern emerging
like the back of a rug.
The tender seedlings
raise their pinheads
with the cap of seed stuck on.
Cruel and smiling with sharp
teeth is the love of lettuce.
You grow out of last year's
composted dinner and you
will end up in my hot mouth.
—MARGE PIERCY

HERB GARDEN

I know a garden with a loveliness
Deeper than eye can see or indrawn breath
Can measure rightly. Ancient centuries press
Against its walls till time is gone and death
Is lost in fragrance of the lavender
That grows serenely by a lichened stile.
Basil, rosemary, marjoram are there,
And savory, whose blossoms lift a smile
Beside a dripping pool. There silver sage
And lads-love, that all our mothers knew
And pressed for us in many a yellowed page.
Woodruff is there, mint, caraway, and rue.
Old flowers are lovely, lovelier still are these
Sweet-scented herbs near box and cedar trees.
— CATHERINE CATE COBLENTZ

A Fruit-Piece

The afternoon of summer folds
Its warm arms round the marigolds,
And, with its gleaming fingers, pets
The watered pinks and violets

That from the casement vases spill,
Over the cottage window-sill,
Their fragrance down the garden walks
Where droop the dry-mouthed hollyhocks.

How vividly the sunshine scrawls
The grape-vine shadows on the walls!
How like a truant swings the breeze
In high boughs of the apple-trees!

The slender "free-stone" lifts aloof,
Full languidly above the roof,

A hoard of fruitage, stamped with gold
And precious mintings manifold.

High up, through curled green leaves, a pear
Hangs hot with ripeness here and there.
Beneath the sagging trellisings,
In lush, lack-luster clusterings,

Great torpid grapes, all fattened through
With moon and sunshine, shade and dew,
Until their swollen girths express
But forms of limp deliciousness—

Drugged to an indolence divine
With heaven's own sacramental wine.
—JAMES WHITCOMB RILEY

PUMPKINS

At the end of the garden,
Across the litter of weeds and grass cuttings,
The pumpkin spreads its coarse,
Bristled, hollow-stemmed lines,
Erupting in great leaves
Above flowers
The nobbly and prominent
Stigmas of which
Are like fuses
Waiting to be set by bees.

When, like a string
Of yellow mines
Across the garden,
The pumpkins will smolder
And swell,
Drawing the combustion from the sun
To make their own.
At night I lie
Waiting for detonations,
Half expecting
To find the garden
Cratered like a moon.

—JOHN COTTON

THE GERANIUM

If you wish to grow a lily
　　With its white and golden hue,
You will have to have a mansion
　　And a gardener or two.

A rose must have a radiant bush
　　With lots of room and air;
And a peony wants the terrace
　　Of a multimillionaire;

But all a poor geranium
　　Will ever ask a man–
Is a little bit of fragrant earth
　　And an old tomato can.

—LEONARD FEENEY

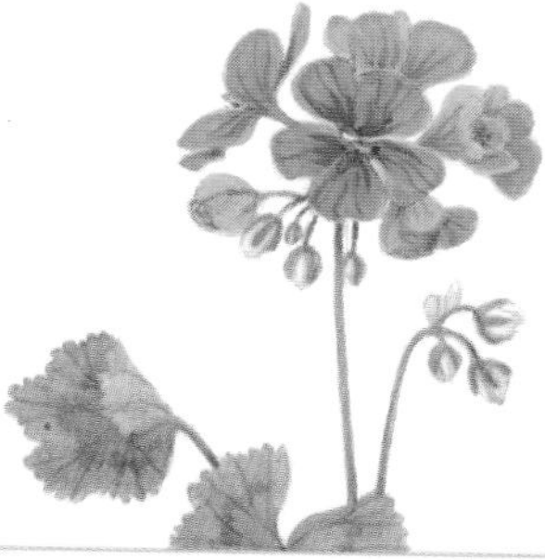

MY WINDOW GARDEN

I have a little garden box
Upon my windowsill,
Where hyacinths and sedums grow
And lilies bloom at will.

No matter how the winter's storms
May rage with ghoulish glee
And beat against my casement there,
It never frightens me.

I watch my flowers from day to day,
I water them with care
And they give back their sweet perfume —
Their fragrance fills the air.

I wonder if in years to come
That window box will grow,
When I who tend it now so well
Shall sleep beneath the snow?

I wonder if—but who can tell
What passing years may bring?
But still—there's always flowers to bloom
And always birds to sing.
—IVA H. DREW

MARIGOLDS

Do you like marigolds? If you do
Then my garden is gay for you!
I've been cutting their fragrant stalks
Where they lean on the garden walks.

The head's too heavy for the brittle stem,
A careless touch and you've broken them.
Each one shines like a separate star
Set in some heaven where gardens are.

My hands smell of the herb-like scent,
Telling what garden way I went.
Pungent, vivid and strong, they stay
Long after summer has gone away.

Do you like marigolds? Here's a pledge
To meet the frost with a golden edge —
To go as far as a weak thing may
Linking tomorrow with yesterday.
— LOUISE DRISCOLL

Violets

Under the green hedges, after the snow,
There do the dear little violets grow;
Hiding their modest and beautiful heads
Under the hawthorn in soft mossy beds.

Sweet as the roses and blue as the sky,
Down there do the dear little violets lie;
Hiding their heads where they scarce may be seen,
By the leaves you may know where the violet hath been.
—John Moultrie

POPPIES

The strange, bright dancers
Are in the garden.
The wind of summer
Is a soft music.
Scarlet and orange,
Flaming and golden,
The strange, bright dancers
Move to the music.
And some are whiter
Than snow in winter,
And float like snowflakes
Drifting the garden.
Oh, have you seen them,
The strange, bright dancers,
Nodding and swaying
To the wind's music?

— P. A. ROPES

ROSES

You love the roses—so do I. I wish
The sky would rain down roses, as they rain
From off the shaken bush. Why will it not?
Then all the valley would be pink and white
And soft to tread on. They would fall as light
As feathers, smelling sweet: and it would be
Like sleeping and yet waking, all at once.

—GEORGE ELIOT

HOLLYHOCKS

Old-fashioned flowers! I love them all:
The morning-glories on the wall,
The pansies in their patch of shade,
The violets, stolen from a glade,
The bleeding hearts and columbine,
Have long been garden friends of mine;
But memory every summer flocks
About a clump of hollyhocks.

The mother loved them years ago;
Beside the fence they used to grow,
And though the garden changed each year
And certain blooms would disappear

To give their places in the ground
To something new that mother found,
Some pretty bloom or rosebush rare —
The hollyhocks were always there.

It seems but yesterday to me
She led me down the yard to see
The first tall spires, with bloom aflame,
And taught me to pronounce their name.
And when today their blooms I see,
Always the mother smiles at me;
The mind's bright chambers, life unlocks
Each summer with the hollyhocks.

—EDGAR A. GUEST

ROSE AND ROOT

The Rose aloft in sunny air,
   Beloved alike by bird and bee,
Takes for the dark Root little care
   That toils below it ceaselessly.

I put my question to the flower:
   "Pride of the Summer, garden queen,
Why livest thou thy little hour?"
   And the Rose answered, "I am seen."

I put my question to the Root,
   "I mine the earth content," it said.
"A hidden miner underfoot;
   I know a Rose is overhead."
   —JOHN JAMES PIATT

TITLE INDEX

Author Index

First Line Index

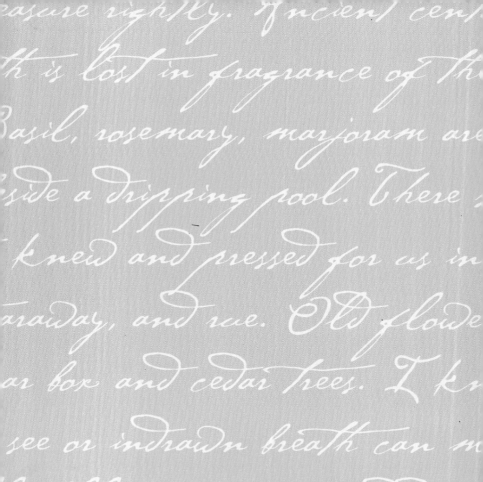